John Adams

Second U.S. President

Colonial Leaders

Lord Baltimore
English Politician and Colonist

Benjamin Banneker
American Mathematician and Astronomer

Sir William Berkeley
Governor of Virginia

William Bradford
Governor of Plymouth Colony

Jonathan Edwards
Colonial Religious Leader

Benjamin Franklin
American Statesman, Scientist, and Writer

Anne Hutchinson
Religious Leader

Cotton Mather
Author, Clergyman, and Scholar

Increase Mather
Clergyman and Scholar

James Oglethorpe
Humanitarian and Soldier

William Penn
Founder of Democracy

Sir Walter Raleigh
English Explorer and Author

Caesar Rodney
American Patriot

John Smith
English Explorer and Colonist

Miles Standish
Plymouth Colony Leader

Peter Stuyvesant
Dutch Military Leader

George Whitefield
Clergyman and Scholar

Roger Williams
Founder of Rhode Island

John Winthrop
Politician and Statesman

John Peter Zenger
Free Press Advocate

Revolutionary War Leaders

John Adams
Second U.S. President

Ethan Allen
Revolutionary Hero

Benedict Arnold
Traitor to the Cause

King George III
English Monarch

Nathanael Greene
Military Leader

Nathan Hale
Revolutionary Hero

Alexander Hamilton
First U.S. Secretary of the Treasury

John Hancock
President of the Continental Congress

Patrick Henry
American Statesman and Speaker

John Jay
First Chief Justice of the Supreme Court

Thomas Jefferson
Author of the Declaration of Independence

John Paul Jones
Father of the U.S. Navy

Lafayette
French Freedom Fighter

James Madison
Father of the Constitution

Francis Marion
The Swamp Fox

James Monroe
American Statesman

Thomas Paine
Political Writer

Paul Revere
American Patriot

Betsy Ross
American Patriot

George Washington
First U.S. President

Famous Figures of the Civil War Era

Jefferson Davis
Confederate President

Frederick Douglass
Abolitionist and Author

Ulysses S. Grant
Military Leader and President

Stonewall Jackson
Confederate General

Robert E. Lee
Confederate General

Abraham Lincoln
Civil War President

William Sherman
Union General

Harriet Beecher Stowe
Author of Uncle Tom's Cabin

Sojourner Truth
Abolitionist, Suffragist, and Preacher

Harriet Tubman
Leader of the Underground Railroad

John Adams

Second U.S. President

Michael Burgan

Arthur M. Schlesinger, jr.
Senior Consulting Editor

Chelsea House Publishers

Philadelphia

Produced by 21st Century Publishing and Communications, Inc.
New York, NY. http://www.21cpc.com

CHELSEA HOUSE PUBLISHERS
Production Manager Pamela Loos
Art Director Sara Davis
Director of Photography Judy L. Hasday
Managing Editor James D. Gallagher
Senior Production Editor J. Christopher Higgins

Staff for *JOHN ADAMS*
Project Editor/Publishing Coordinator Jim McAvoy
Project Editor Anne Hill
Associate Art Director Takeshi Takahashi
Series Design Keith Trego

The Chelsea House World Wide Web address is
http://www.chelseahouse.com

First Printing
1 3 5 7 9 8 6 4 2

Library of Congress Cataloging-in-Publication Data

Burgan, Michael.
    John Adams / Michael Burgan.
        p.   cm. — (Revolutionary War leaders)
    Includes bibliographical references and index.
    ISBN 0-7910-5970-7 (hc) — 0-7910-6128-0 (pbk.)
    1. Adams, John, 1735-1826—Juvenile literature. 2. Presidents—
    United States—Biography—Juvenile literature. [1. Adams, John,
    1735-1826. 2. Presidents.] I. Title. II. Series.

    E322.B836 2000
    973.4'4'092—dc21
    [B]   00-038390
                                                               CIP

Publisher's Note: In Colonial and Revolutionary War America,
there were no standard rules for spelling, punctuation, capitaliza-
tion, or grammar. Some of the quotations that appear in the Colonial Leaders and Revolutionary War Leaders series come from
original documents and letters written during this time in history.
Original quotations reflect writing inconsistencies of the period.

Contents

Like these colonists, who are on their way to church, John's family left their home country–England–and came to America to practice their religion freely. John also learned his first lessons about hard work and honesty at church.

First Lessons

Orchards, fields, and farms dotted the countryside in Braintree, Massachusetts. This small town south of Boston was the home of John and Susanna Adams. The couple were respected citizens of Braintree. Susanna came from a good family–her father was a doctor. John worked hard on his farm during the summers, then made shoes during the winters. He also was a member of the local **militia**, a group of citizens prepared to serve as soldiers during an emergency. John was active in the church as well. He served as a deacon, or leader, and was sometimes called "Deacon John."

The Adams family came from a long line of Puritans, the English people who had settled most of Massachusetts. The first Puritans arrived in the 1630s. They had come to America so they could worship as they pleased. In England, their religion was restricted by the government. In America, the Puritans were still ruled by the king of England, but they could follow their own religion and run their local government. People such as John and Susanna Adams valued this freedom. They also believed in the importance of hard work and honesty.

On October 30, 1735, Deacon John and Susanna Adams had their first child. They named him John. They taught him their Puritan beliefs and the value of learning.

When little John was about six, he went to a local school. He learned little rhymes such as "He who ne'er learns his ABC, forever will a blockhead be." John was no blockhead, but he was easily bored with his lessons. John later wrote that he wanted to spend as much time as he could

John went to a small, one-room school much like this one. But he preferred spending time playing outside rather than being indoors.

"making and sailing boats and Ships upon the Ponds and Brooks, in making and flying Kites, in driving hoops, playing marbles. . . Wrestling, Swimming, Skaiting, and above all in shooting. . . . "

John loved the outdoors and hoped to someday take over his father's farm. Deacon John had other plans. He wanted his son to go to Harvard College. One day John went with his father to the fields. He wanted to show his father he could be a good farmer. After a hard day's work, Mr. Adams asked his son how he enjoyed farming.

"I like it very well, sir," John said.

"Ay but I don't like it so well," replied his father. "So you shall go to school." After John grew up he would win many arguments, but he could not win this one with his father.

When he was 15, John Adams set off for Harvard. The school is located in Cambridge, just across the river from Boston. Only young men went to college in those days. Most went when they were John's age. They studied Latin, Greek, math, and science. John's father wanted him to be a minister, but John had other ideas. His friends at school were impressed with his fine speaking talents. They told him he should be a lawyer.

John thought it might be good to practice law. He could make more money then he could as a minister. He could also win fame. By the time he was 20, John felt a need to earn "Honour or Reputation" during his life. He did not want to

Many young men like John received their education at Harvard College, which was established in 1636 in Massachusetts. They usually studied Latin, Greek, math, and science.

be like "the common Herd of Mankind, who are to be born and eat and sleep and die, and be forgotten."

John graduated from Harvard in 1755. His first job was teaching at a school in Worcester, a town about 60 miles west of Boston. About a year after he arrived there, he also began studying law. When he was not working, John spent time talking about politics. Britain and France were fighting the French and Indian War. This war had a large impact on the American colonies.

John also did a lot of thinking about how people should live a good life. "Honesty, Sincerity and Openness, I esteem essential marks of a good mind," he wrote in 1756. He believed that people should choose their beliefs carefully, then "defend them with boldness." John was referring to religion, but he defended his political beliefs just as strongly in the years to come.

John completed his law

During the 1750s, Britain and France fought to control North America. Native Americans often joined these battles. The fighting turned into a war known as the French and Indian War (1754–1763).

In 1754, a young colonel named George Washington led British troops in battles against the French. Five years later, the British forced the French to leave North America. The fighting continued in Europe, and Great Britain needed money to defend its North American lands. The Americans and British argued over new taxes. This conflict led to the American Revolution.

studies in three years. He then traveled to Boston to start his own practice in 1758. He slowly found clients, and in 1760 he won his first case in front of a jury. He also became friendly with some of the most important Boston lawyers of the day. One of these men was James Otis Jr. In 1761, Otis argued a case that had a strong effect on the American colonies.

The English lawmakers in Parliament wanted to raise more taxes in America. One way to do this was to collect **duties** on certain goods. For many years, smuggling had been common in Boston. **Merchants** secretly brought in goods to avoid paying the duties. But now Parliament ordered the Massachusetts government to give out documents called **writs of assistance**. These writs let the authorities search for smuggled goods wherever they wanted.

The Boston merchants thought the writs were illegal. They believed officials could not search a person's home without a specific reason. The debate over the writs went to court. James Otis spoke for the Boston merchants. With great anticipation, John attended the trial. He wanted to take notes on what Otis said. Otis spoke powerfully for nearly five hours—so powerfully, John sometimes forgot to write. He was too busy listening to what Otis had to say.

"Now one of the most essential branches of English liberty," Otis argued, "is the freedom of one's house. A man's house is his castle, and while he is quiet, he is as well guarded as a prince in his castle." Otis said that Parliament had no legal power to pass the law ordering the writs. The law went against a basic set of guaranteed rights. Otis called these basic rights a **constitution**. This constitution was not a written document. It was the total of English laws and politics as they had developed over the centuries.

Otis lost his case, and the Massachusetts government issued the writs. But Otis had spoken out about the rights of the colonists. His ideas led others to think about whether Parliament

At the beginning of John Adams's law career, he was inspired by the arguments of another Boston lawyer, James Otis.

could pass any laws that affected the rights of Americans. Otis's words in the court also inspired John. Years later, John wrote, "Then and there the child Independence was born." But at that time, John, like most Americans, had no thoughts of the American colonies breaking free from Britain.

John inherited a small, quiet farm like this one from his father. John was always happy to be away from politics and able to work on the land.

The Resistance Grows

J ohn Adams wanted success in his legal career. But part of him still longed to be a farmer. He finally got the chance to work the land after his father died in May 1761. John inherited a small house and 10 acres of farmland. He quickly threw himself into farming. In 1762 he wrote about his busy farm life: "Sometimes I am at the orchard Ploughing up Acre after Acre and Planting, pruning Apple Trees, mending fences. . . . " John's interest in agriculture led to his first published articles. They appeared in a Boston newspaper, the *Gazette*. Using the name "Humphrey Ploughjogger," John wrote amusing pieces about farming. Sometimes he also commented on the politics of the day.

During this period of his life, John also found time to start a family. In October 1764, he married 20-year-old Abigail Smith, who was from nearby Weymouth. John was struck by Abigail's "million Charms and Graces." The couple had met a few years earlier. Their relationship grew stronger as they dated and exchanged long letters. They would continue to write each other often for the rest of their lives. The letters of Abigail Adams later became an important resource for historians. They provided details about her husband and their life in the early days of the United States.

John and his wife lived in the small cottage on his farm. Within a year, the couple had a daughter. They named her Abigail, but most people called her Nabby. She was the first of five Adams children. By this time, John was getting more work for his law practice and he traveled to courts all over Massachusetts. He

John's wife, Abigail Adams, wrote letters to her husband which give interesting details about life in colonial times.

also found himself being drawn into politics. A new crisis with Great Britain was sweeping across the colonies.

Since 1763, Great Britain had tried to collect

more money from the American colonies. In 1764, the British Parliament passed the Sugar Act. This law increased taxes on some items and added new taxes on others. The taxed goods included cloth, coffee, wine, and sugar. At the same time, Great Britain worked harder to collect other taxes already in place.

In America some colonists grumbled to one another about the Sugar Act. But the protests grew somewhat louder in 1765, with the passage of the Stamp Act. This time Parliament wanted to tax all printed materials used in the colonies. These included newspapers, legal documents, insurance policies–even playing cards. The new tax affected just about everyone, including some of the most powerful people in the colonies, such as merchants, lawyers, and publishers.

The vocal opponents of the Stamp Act said Parliament had no right to collect the Stamp Act tax. They saw a difference between this kind of tax and a tax on goods brought into the colonies. Some critics went on to say that Parliament could not pass any tax on the Americans because the Americans did not have political representation in Parliament. The colonists believed they had the same rights as people living in Great Britain. But unlike those British citizens, the Americans were not allowed to vote in elections to choose their **representatives** in Parliament. No one argued against some kind of tax on the colonies. But John's friend, James Otis, said, "Taxation without representation is **tyranny**."

The anger against the Stamp Act soon led to violence in some colonies. In Boston, Samuel Adams, John's cousin, helped form a group called the Sons of

Guy Fawkes Day is a holiday in Great Britain. People celebrate a failed attempt to blow up Parliament in 1605. During colonial times, gangs of young men in Boston fought each other on Guy Fawkes Day. But these gangs worked together in August 1765, when a group called the Sons of Liberty recruited the young men to help protest the Stamp Act.

The gangs stormed the house of Andrew Oliver, the stamp agent in Boston. In his diary, John Adams wrote how the angry crowd broke into Oliver's house. "His furniture [was] destroyed and his whole family [was] thrown into Confusion and Terror."

**John's cousin, Samuel Adams, was a founder
of the Sons of Liberty in Boston and a signer
of the Declaration of Independence.**

Liberty. The members of the group were sometimes called patriots. The patriots led protests
against the Stamp Act. The protests often turned

violent. John strongly opposed the Stamp Act, but he did not like the violence against it either.

As the protests went on, John wrote about the political issues of the day. He described his idea of a perfect government. It would be "mixed," with three distinct branches: one branch would make laws (**legislative**); one would carry out the laws (**executive**); and one would make sure the laws were applied fairly (**judicial**). This system was later used by many state governments and the national government of the United States. John also argued against taxation without representation.

The Stamp Act was scheduled to take effect on November 1, 1765. In October, nine colonies, including Massachusetts, sent representatives to New York to discuss the options. At this "Stamp Act Congress," the colonies agreed to band together and demand that Parliament **repeal**, or eliminate, the tax. To protest the tax, some of the colonies also decided to **boycott** goods that came from Great Britain.

When November 1 came, none of the stamp agents in the colonies were willing to collect the tax. They were too afraid of the angry colonists. In response the British government shut down the courts and port in Boston. Six weeks later, John Adams was one of three lawyers picked to represent Boston. The representatives' job was to convince the Massachusetts governor to reopen the courts. The governor refused, which meant that John and all of the other lawyers in the area could not practice law.

In the spring of 1766, the colonies learned that Parliament had decided to repeal the Stamp Act because the American boycott of British goods was hurting British merchants too badly. The delighted Americans celebrated their great victory. Parliament, though, still claimed it had the right to collect future taxes. John could see that the Stamp Act crisis had stirred up very strong feelings in the colonies. More people, he believed, were "more attentive to their liberties and more determined to defend them." Those feelings continued to grow.

For a short while after the Stamp Act crisis, the colonies were calm. But once again in 1767, Parliament passed new taxes on America. These taxes were called the Townshend Acts. The new taxes sparked more protests against taxation without representation. Samuel Adams tried to convince his cousin John to be more active in fighting against the British. John was not ready to do so. He was afraid it would hurt his growing law practice. But he did agree with the patriots' goals. So he helped them in secret, writing some materials for them. John also believed that the British would continue to try to restrict the freedom of Americans.

John demonstrated his growing devotion to the cause in 1768. That summer, an old friend named Jonathan Sewall approached John and offered him a position as a lawyer, working for the governor of Massachusetts. The job would have meant much more money. Throughout his career, John worried that he did not make enough money to support his family. But he did not need any time to consider this offer. John flatly refused the job. He told Sewall he could not work for a government that passed laws which went against "all my Ideas of Right, Justice, and Policy."

That fall, British soldiers arrived in Boston, where John and his family were now living. The soldiers came to make sure the taxes were collected and to prevent any more violence. To the British, Boston was the major spot of colonial protests. Some mornings, John heard the British soldiers marching in front of his house.

As time went by, many people in Boston grew to hate the British soldiers around them. The soldiers wore long, red coats, so some citizens called them "lobster backs" and "redcoats." Young boys sometimes threw stones at the troops. Extreme tension between the soldiers and the patriots grew rapidly. Then, finally, the tensions exploded into violence.

On the night of March 5, 1770, John was meeting with some friends. He later wrote, "About nine [o'clock] We were allarmed with the ringing of Bells, and supposing it to be the Signal of fire, we snatched our Hats and Cloaks . . . and went out to assist in quenching the fire or aiding our friends who might be in danger." But nothing was on fire. John soon learned why the people had been called out by the bells. A group of British soldiers had fired shots at a large mob. The people had been teasing the soldiers and throwing coal and snowballs at them. When the soldiers fired, they killed three people. Two others later died of their wounds.

Soon all of Boston was talking about the event, and people were calling it the "Boston Massacre." The soldiers and their officer, Captain Thomas Preston, faced murder trials. Preston approached several lawyers to defend him and eight of his soldiers. All of the lawyers refused to take the case, except for John. He was concerned about being called a "Tory"—a supporter of the British.

On March 5, 1770, British soldiers fired into a crowd of unarmed colonial citizens, killing five. John later defended eight of the British soldiers in court.

The patriots might have even decided to attack him because he took the case and was defending the hated British soldiers. But that fear did not stop him. He believed everyone, including British soldiers, deserved a fair trial.

John managed to have the trial postponed. This gave him more time to prepare his case. It also helped cool down the fiery feelings against the redcoats. The case went to court in October. John argued that Preston had not ordered his men to fire. He also claimed that the soldiers who did shoot were acting to protect themselves from the mob. John said, "If an assault was made to endanger their lives, the law is clear, they had a right to kill in their own defence."

His arguments were convincing. Preston and six of the eight soldiers were found innocent. The other two soldiers were convicted of a lesser crime, but not murder. John Adams believed he had done Boston a great service with his handling of this case. He had shown that following the law was more important than giving in to heated emotions. But within a few years, strong emotions once again flared in Boston.

To protest the tax on tea, some American colonists disguised themselves as Native Americans, boarded ships that came from England, and dumped chests of tea into Boston Harbor. The event became known as the Boston Tea Party.

The Road to War

After the Boston Massacre, Parliament decided to give in to the colonists a little. The British government repealed most of the taxes that had been part of the Townshend Acts. But they kept a tax on one important item: tea. During the 18th century, tea was one of the most popular drinks in America. After the British taxed it, some merchants began smuggling tea. Other people tried to stop drinking it.

By 1773, the smuggling and efforts to reduce tea drinking began to have an effect. The East India Company, which controlled the tea trade, was losing money. Parliament passed special laws designed to help the company. Parliament also said tea would now be taxed only in America and not in Great Britain.

Once again, the patriots were angry. They saw the new tea law as another unfair tax on the colonies. In Boston, Samuel Adams led the fight to keep tea out of the city. In November, the first of three ships arrived from England carrying crates of tea. The patriots asked the governor, Thomas Hutchinson, to send the ships back to England. He refused. Finally, on the night of December 16, a crowd of patriots stormed the ships. Some of the men were partially disguised as Native Americans. The patriots threw all the tea into the harbor. This act of protest became known as the Boston Tea Party.

John Adams did not take part in this "party," but he supported it.

The tea party angered the British government, which soon sent General Thomas Gage to take over as governor of Massachusetts. Parliament also sent more troops to Boston and closed the port. New laws limited the power of the local governments throughout the colonies. The Americans were even ordered to take British soldiers into their homes. The colonists decided it was time to act together against the British.

In September 1774, **delegates** from 12 of the 13 colonies (all except Georgia) met in Philadelphia. The meeting was called the Continental Congress. John Adams was one of the delegates from Massachusetts. At the Continental Congress, John was on the committee that debated what the colonies should do.

Almost everyone was against taxation without representation. But the delegates argued over what specific rights the Americans had. In the end, the committee agreed that the recent laws passed by Parliament were unconstitutional and that colonists should not obey them. Until Parliament repealed the laws, the colonies would boycott British goods. The colonies also made plans to train their own militias and agreed on a list of the political rights held by Americans.

In October, John was chosen to write the final document. It was called the Declaration of Rights and **Grievances**. During his weeks in Philadelphia, John started to emerge as an important political leader of the colonies.

A few months later, John wrote a series of articles. The articles explained why Parliament should listen to the colonies before passing laws that affected Americans. John claimed he was not for independence. He said, "The patriots . . . wish only to keep their old privileges." Those privileges were their rights as British citizens. But John also knew becoming independent might be the only way to preserve those rights in America.

In Great Britain, the actions of the First Continental Congress stirred a strong response. The colonies had chosen to defy Parliament and the British king, George III. The British government decided to take action, fearing it might lose control of America forever. The government

**British troops marching into Boston. After the
Boston Tea Party, the British government sent more
troops to Boston and closed the port.**

ordered General Gage to move against the
rebellious colony of Massachusetts.

In April 1775, British troops marched to
Concord. They planned to arrest patriot leaders
and seize the guns and ammunition stored there.

Massachusetts militiamen confronted the red-coats in the town of Lexington. Shots rang out, and eight Americans were killed. The fighting continued in Concord and on the road back to Boston. By the time the day was over, more than 70 British soldiers were dead. The colonies had taken their first step toward armed revolution.

Not long thereafter, the Second Continental Congress met in Philadelphia. The situation was very serious. However, John and the other delegates could not agree on what should be done. Even after the fighting in Massachusetts, some Americans still hoped to end the crisis peacefully. A few delegates in Philadelphia hoped the colonies could remain part of Great Britain. But through the rest of 1775 and into 1776, the war grew. British and American troops fought more battles in Mass-achusetts, and new fighting broke out in New York, Canada, and Virginia.

One of the first actions taken by Congress was to name George Washington the commander of the American forces. John suggested this move in June 1775. The two men had met at the First Continental Congress and John was impressed by Washington's "excellent universal Character." After Washington took charge, his troops drove the redcoats out of Boston.

John suggested the colonies should set up their own governments. He believed they should act as independent states united to fight against the British.

By June 1776, the British were planning a massive attack on New York. Congress had to make its next move. More of the delegates now began to favor declaring their independence from Great Britain, and John was one of the leading supporters of the idea. On June 7, Virginia delegate Richard Henry Lee made a formal request that Congress declare independence. John supported Lee's request. Two days later John wrote, "We are in the very midst of a revolution, the most complete, unexpected, and remarkable, of any in the history of nations."

Still, not all the delegates were ready to vote for independence yet. Some had not received instructions from the government of their states. Congress decided to wait a few weeks before voting. In the meantime, a committee of five delegates would draft a document declaring independence for Congress to consider. John was one of the members of the committee. The others were Roger Sherman of Connecticut, Robert Livingston of New York, Benjamin Franklin of Pennsylvania, and Thomas Jefferson of Virginia.

When the committee met, John suggested that Jefferson should actually write the declaration because Jefferson "had the reputation of a masterly pen." John also believed it was important to have someone from Virginia take the lead so the British would see all Americans supported independence, not just the rebels in Massachusetts.

To write this important document, Jefferson borrowed ideas from well-known political thinkers of the day and asked John and Benjamin Franklin for comments. On July 1 the committee presented a draft of the declaration to Congress. The document said that King George III had trampled on the legal rights of Americans. Because of this, the Americans were declaring their independence and they were forming a new nation: the United States of America.

The delegates heatedly debated the document. John Dickinson of Pennsylvania spoke against independence. "I know the name of liberty is dear to each one of us," he said. "But have we not enjoyed liberty even under the English monarchy?"

There was a long silence. No one responded to Dickinson's comment. Then John rose to speak. He spoke slowly at first, collecting his thoughts. By the time he was done he had talked for more than two hours. Some historians have called this the greatest speech of John's life. What he said was not recorded. Jefferson later said that John's words had a "power . . . that moved us from our seats." John later compared himself to the great speakers of ancient Greece and Rome. None of them, he said, "ever had

**John Adams (left, with hand on hip) and other members
of the committee look on as Thomas Jefferson presents the
Declaration of Independence to the Continental Congress.**

before him a question of more Importance to his
Country and to the World."

John convinced the delegates to accept the
Declaration of Independence. Congress made
some minor changes and the final version was

approved on July 4, 1776. Four days later, it was read publicly for the first time. In Philadelphia, people cheered and bells rang as the Americans learned about their independence.

During the debate over independence, John wrote to Abigail back in Massachusetts. His words probably expressed what many Americans felt when they heard the Declaration of Independence. "I am well aware," he wrote, "of the toil, and blood, and treasure, that it will cost us to maintain this declaration . . . yet, through all the gloom, I can see the rays of ravishing light and glory."

On July 3, 1776, John Adams wrote Abigail about the events of July 2. On that day, Congress voted to declare independence. John predicted July 2 "will be celebrated . . . as the great anniversary festival." He thought Americans should honor the day "with pomp and parade, with shows, games, sports, guns, bells, bonfires, and illuminations, from one end of this continent to the other, from this time forward forevermore." John was partly right—people did wildly celebrate the anniversary of independence. But the holiday came on July 4, the day Congress approved the Declaration of Independence, not July 2.

American troops lay siege to a British fort. In the early days of the Revolutionary War, both the colonial forces and the British troops suffered heavy losses.

4

Service at Home and Abroad

Not all Americans welcomed the Declaration of Independence. Some people preferred to remain part of Great Britain. Across the new country, popular opinion was split into three groups: people eagerly supporting independence; people actively against it; and people who were not sure what to do.

But the government of the new nation had a clear mission: to win independence on the battlefield. John was put in charge of the Board of War and Ordnance, which directed the war effort for America. With this job and his other duties, John often worked from before dawn until late at night.

The fighting did not go well for the Americans in the weeks following the signing of the Declaration of Independence. On Long Island, in New York, Washington's troops suffered a major loss. Afterward, the British general, William Howe, sent a message to Congress to discuss ending the rebellion. John, Benjamin Franklin, and Edward Rutledge were chosen to meet with Howe and his brother, Admiral Richard Howe.

On September 11, 1776, the Americans and the British met on Staten Island. Admiral Howe told the Americans he could only treat them as British subjects, not as representatives from an independent

The trip John took in 1776 to meet with the British in New York had its humorous moments. He and Franklin had to share a small bed at an inn. During the night, the two great leaders argued over whether they should sleep with the window open or shut. John was afraid of catching a cold if the window was open. Franklin argued that no one could get sick from cold air. John finally opened the window, then jumped into the bed, as Franklin continued to talk. John later wrote, "I soon fell asleep, and left him and his Philosophy together."

country. John angrily replied, "Your lordship may consider me, in what light you please . . . *except that of a British Subject.*" The three patriots had no intention of giving in. As the conversation went on, John realized that the two sides could not peacefully end the war.

For the next year, John carried out his duties as a member of the Continental Congress. One of his most important goals was improving Washington's army. Soldiers often served only a brief time, then went home. John proposed giving new recruits money or land if they stayed in the army for longer periods.

John took one break from his duties to go home to Braintree. At the end of 1776, he spent about two months with his family before returning to Congress. Both John and his wife knew that he had an important job to do for the country.

During 1777, the war went better for the Americans. Washington and his men won some important victories in New Jersey. But in September, the British took over Philadelphia and

Congress fled the city. The Americans then came back with a major victory at Saratoga, New York. Almost 6,000 British troops surrendered and were sent back to Great Britain. The American victory showed the leaders in European countries that the United States had a chance to win the war. France was by then ready to increase its aid to the Americans and send French soldiers to fight alongside them.

In November 1777, Congress named John Adams a U.S. representative to France. As a **diplomat**, John hoped to obtain more aid from the French. Early the following year, John and his son John Quincy Adams set sail for France. The voyage was difficult as storms stirred the seas. When father and son reached Paris, they joined two other American diplomats—Benjamin Franklin and Arthur Lee.

In some ways, John was not a good diplomat. Diplomacy requires saying just the right thing to powerful people. John had no experience dealing with foreign leaders, and he found it hard to

The British surrender of 6,000 men at Saratoga, New York, was a great victory for the colonial army.

get along with people he did not know. Some people considered John rude, while others thought he was too formal. But he had other qualities that were useful for a diplomat. He was intelligent and devoted to his country. And he understood the need for the United States to win support from other nations.

Benjamin Franklin was very popular in Paris. John worked with Franklin to get more money from the French, which was needed to help the colonial army win the war with Britain.

John handled the U.S. diplomats' paperwork and he attended meetings with French leaders. But Franklin was the favorite and John remained in the background. In December 1778, Congress decided to make Franklin the only U.S. diplomat in France. A few months later, John and his son returned to the town of Braintree.

Back home, John entered local politics again. Massachusetts was about to create its first state constitution. Braintree selected John to be its representative at a constitutional **convention**. John was asked to write the constitution. His draft reflected his ideas on government and was at the heart of the final document, which was approved in 1780. But once again, John stayed in Braintree only briefly. Soon he was back in Europe, again as a diplomat.

Congress sent John to France to prepare for future peace talks with Great Britain. The war was going well for the Americans. The British were also fighting France and Spain at the same time, so the American leaders believed Parliament would soon want to end the war in America.

John arrived in France in early 1780. He did not trust the French foreign minister, who was clearly looking out for France's interests alone. But John could not afford to offend America's only strong foreign ally.

John realized that the war would not end soon. He traveled to the Netherlands, arriving in August 1780. John stayed there more than two years. During that time, he convinced the Dutch government to loan money to the United States. The Dutch also agreed to recognize America as an independent nation. John said that moment "gave me more satisfaction" than the Declaration of Independence.

In October 1781, the United States won a major victory at Yorktown, Virginia. The battle convinced Parliament that the British could not win the war and the Americans would get their independence. All that was left to do was sign a peace treaty. One year later, John left Amsterdam for Paris. He, Franklin, and John Jay were America's representatives at the peace talks.

The talks went on for weeks. John wanted to make sure Great Britain would honor America's independence after the treaty was signed. He also watched the French carefully; he still did not trust them to serve American interests.

John was one of the signers of the Treaty of Paris in 1783, which officially ended the American Revolution.

Finally, in January 1783, all the countries agreed on a first draft of the peace treaty. The document was called the Treaty of Paris.

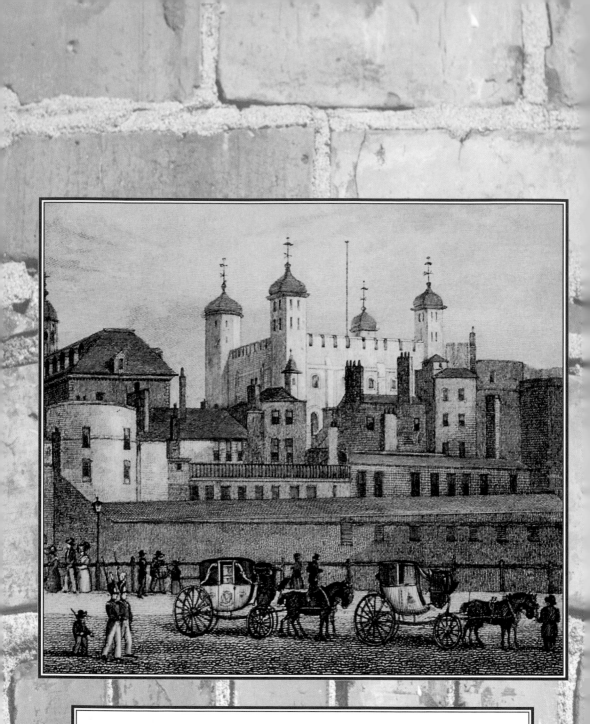

John and his family lived in the busy city of London
while he served as the first U.S. ambassador to Britain.

On to the Presidency

After the Treaty of Paris was signed, John Adams remained in Europe. He traveled for a short while in England and returned briefly to the Netherlands. The United States once again needed a loan from the Dutch government. In the summer of 1784, Abigail and Nabby joined John in England. The family then headed for France, where they lived for about eight months. The next spring, John took on a new role for his government. He traveled to London as the first U.S. minister, or ambassador, to Great Britain.

Within a few days, John visited King George III.

Just a few years before, John had been a rebellious British subject. He could have been arrested and sent to prison for disobeying the king. Now he stood before King George representing the free nation of the United States. John said to the king, "I think myself more fortunate than all my fellow-citizens, in having the distinguished honor to be the first to stand in your Majesty's royal presence in a diplomatic character." The king told John that he hoped for friendly relations between the two nations.

During his time in London, John struggled to convince the British to keep the agreements made in the Treaty of Paris. But British officials tended to ignore his pleas. At one point John told John Jay that the "popular pulse seems to beat high against America." John also took time off from his work, traveling throughout Great Britain with his wife.

John renewed his friendship with Thomas Jefferson, who was serving as minister to France at the time. The Adams family had grown close

Thomas Jefferson was John's good friend, even though they sometimes disagreed about politics.

to Jefferson during their time in France. In London, both John and Abigail Adams wrote many letters to Jefferson. When Jefferson traveled to London in 1786, he visited the Adamses often.

Back in America, the young country was struggling to keep its government running smoothly. Since 1781, the United States had been operating under the Articles of Confederation. This document had created a weak national government. The individual states had most of the power. Many political leaders saw the need for a new, more powerful national government. Representatives from each state once again met in Philadelphia at the Constitutional Convention in 1787 to decide how to organize the new government.

Although John did not attend this convention, some of his political ideas were included in the final document, which was called the Constitution. John had written a work called *A Defence of the Constitutions of Governments of the United States of America* the year before. Some of the delegates at the convention had read the first volume of John's work. They also were familiar with John's earlier political ideas. The delegates used many of John's ideas as they shaped the Constitution.

The new government was mixed, with three branches: legislative, executive, and judicial, as John had suggested. Each branch was independent of the other two. The whole system, John believed, had to have "checks and balances." This meant one part of government could limit the power of another. John did not agree with everything in the Constitution. He would have given the president more power. But on the whole, John accepted the Constitution and the national government it created. He soon became a member of that new government.

In February 1789, electors from each state voted for the first U.S. president. George Washington won the vote, and John was chosen as vice president. John had returned to America just a few months before. He was disappointed that he had won only 34 out of 138 votes. He thought he deserved more support after all his years of service to his country. Still, John took the job of vice president. He then moved to the nation's capital, which was in New York City at the time.

George Washington (with sword) is sworn in as America's first president. John (right, with hand on hip) became Washington's vice president.

John soon discovered that the vice president had almost no power and nothing to do. He called his position "the most insignificant office" ever created. He did perform some useful services, such as voting to break ties in Congress. But during his eight years as vice president, John was rarely involved in important government decisions.

During these years, American politics began to split into two separate groups, or parties. One party was the Federalists, led by Alexander Hamilton. Hamilton was the first secretary of the treasury. The other party was the Republicans. This party was led by Thomas Jefferson, so they were also known as Jeffersonians. John was a Federalist, but he did not accept all of the party's policies. He was also not close to Hamilton. John began to grow apart from Jefferson as well. Over time, the two old friends held different views about politics. These differences grew into conflicts as John Adams took on a new role.

In 1796, George Washington decided to retire from government service. A number of political leaders sought to replace him as president. John was one of them. The Federalists supported John for president and Thomas Pinckney for vice president. The Republicans backed Jefferson and Aaron Burr. At the time, the president and vice president were chosen from the two candidates with the most electoral votes. A Federalist and a Republican could have been elected to the top two positions. In the end, John beat Jefferson in a close vote and became the second president of America. Jefferson became his vice president.

On March 4, 1797, John Adams was sworn in as president. He wrote to Abigail that he feared the political quarrels between the two political parties would "turn our government topsy-turvy." He had good reason for his fear. Hamilton led a group of Federalists who opposed John. These included members of the president's cabinet, his closest advisors. The Republicans did not support John's policies either.

A major issue of the day was America's relationship with France. The two countries were no longer friendly. The French had recently had their own revolutions and were at war with the British. During this war, France sometimes captured American ships. Many Federalists wanted to go to war with France. But the

Republicans supported the French. John tried to find a balance between these two sides. He wrote, "I dread not a war, with France or England, if either forces it upon US, but [I] will make no Aggression upon either. "

Avoiding war became harder after 1798. The French tried to force three U.S. diplomats to pay a bribe. This "XYZ Affair" led to an undeclared naval war between France and the United States. President Adams feared a larger war might break out. He started to build up the military and raise taxes. He also accepted new laws that tried to limit protests against the government and its actions. These were the Alien and **Sedition** Acts.

These acts limited some freedoms. Many Federalists opposed the number of foreigners in the country. The Federalists believed these immigrants supported the Republicans and wanted good relations with France. The Alien and Sedition Acts made it harder for immigrants to become U.S. citizens. People from "enemy" countries, such as France, could not become citizens at all. These laws also restricted free speech and the freedom of the press. Many people saw the Alien and Sedition Acts as harsh and undemocratic laws.

John later claimed that Hamilton was the major supporter of the Alien and Sedition Acts. He also argued that the government had to act against French spies who were operating in the United States. Still, John was doing his best to avoid an all-out war with France. His approach worked. In 1800 the two countries held peace talks. The threat of a total war against France began to fade.

Hamilton and others were disappointed that the war against the French had not come about. Hamilton continued to oppose John. The president did not help himself in the struggle for influence. He was away from his cabinet too often. The nation's capital had been moved to Philadelphia, but John was spending more time at his home in Braintree, which had since had its name changed to Quincy. John wanted to spend as much time as possible with his dear wife Abigail, who was more frequently sick.

As the election of 1800 neared, the Republicans gained more popular support. Jefferson and Burr ran again for the offices of president and vice president, and the two Republicans each received 73 electoral votes. Eventually the House of Representatives broke the tie and chose Jefferson as president. John had hoped to be reelected, but he finished third. For the first time in more than 25 years, John was out of government service.

John Adams was the first U.S. president to live in the new capital city of Washington, D.C. He moved into the White House in November 1800. At the time, the building was called the President's House. It was not completely done when he arrived. After John spent his first few nights in the empty, damp house alone, he wrote to Abigail that he hoped "none but honest and wise Men ever rule under this roof." Abigail Adams arrived a little later to join her husband. It has been said that she sometimes hung her clothes to dry in one of the large, unfinished rooms.

After he retired, John wrote over 100 letters to Thomas Jefferson. John also wrote many newspaper articles describing his life during the Revolutionary War.

Final Years

John Adams had mixed feelings about his life as a political leader. He told one friend that if he were a young man again, he "would be a Shoemaker rather than an American Statesman." Other times, John seemed bored with his retirement. He told another friend that occasionally he thought about going back into government.

But John stayed out of both state and national politics. Instead, he spent most of his time living quietly in Quincy. He and Abigail called their little home Peacefield. Sometimes their children and grandchildren came to visit them, but they did not have many other guests. Feeling more than a little sad, John told one friend, "I am buried and forgotten." To pass the time, John started working on his autobiography. He wrote small sections between 1802 and 1807 but never really finished the project.

John also wrote to defend his reputation when necessary. An old friend of his, Mercy Otis Warren, wrote a history of the American Revolution. In it, she criticized the political leaders for their behavior after the war. These men, Warren claimed, began to care more about wealth and power than their country. She included John as one of these **corrupt** leaders.

John angrily wrote a series of letters attacking this claim. "I challenge the whole human race," he wrote, "and angels and devils too, to produce an instance of [corrupt behavior] from my cradle to this hour."

John also began writing numerous newspaper articles that described the events of the Revolutionary era in great detail. He wrote other articles that described his time as a diplomat. John spent even more time writing long letters to his old friends. These letters expressed his deep beliefs about life, philosophy, and the current events.

One person John did not write to was Thomas Jefferson. They had disagreed strongly on various political issues when John was president. When John left office and Jefferson started his term, John wrote the new president a letter. Jefferson never responded to him.

Jefferson served as president for eight years. During that time, John did not agree with all of the Republican policies. But in 1812, the two men finally made peace with one another and began to correspond again. John had told some visitors, "I always loved Jefferson and still love him." When Jefferson heard of these kinds words, he and John decided to put aside their political differences. During the next 14 years, John wrote more than 100 letters to Jefferson. They became closer friends than ever before.

As the years passed, more and more of John's friends and relatives died. In 1813, his daughter Nabby died of cancer. Five years later, Abigail died. After her death, John tried to find comfort in his religious beliefs. In a letter to Jefferson, John said he and Abigail "shall meet and know each other in a future State."

John was very pleased with the success of his son, John Quincy. Like his father, John Quincy went to Harvard, became a lawyer, and entered politics. He served as an ambassador to several European nations, a U.S. senator, and secretary of state. In 1825, John Quincy Adams was sworn in as the sixth president of the United States. John said his happy feelings for his son "are too much for a mind like mine, in its ninetieth year."

Even at 90 years old, John was able to enjoy a good meal, a cigar, and talking with his friends. But he knew the end of his life was near. He fought illness in 1825 and into the next year.

John died on the Fourth of July, 50 years after Congress approved the Declaration of Independence.

John had one last wish—to be alive on the 50th anniversary of the day Congress approved the Declaration of Independence. He got his wish.

On July 4, 1826, two great leaders of the American Revolution died just hours apart. In Virginia, Thomas Jefferson died early in the day. The 83-year-old had been sick for more than a week. His last words were "This is the Fourth?" Like John, Jefferson must have known the important anniversary being celebrated that day. John died a few hours later. He did not know Jefferson had already died. John's last words were "Thomas Jefferson survives."

Late in the day on July 4, 1826, John Adams died.

Just a few days earlier, a local official visited Peacefield. He wanted John to suggest a toast for the July 4th celebration. John said, "Independence forever." The man asked if John wanted to add anything else. He replied, "Not a word."

John devoted most of his life to his country. He fought to win freedom for America, and then to preserve his new country's independence. John used his brilliant mind in these struggles. His thoughts and words were as important as the swords and cannons used on the battlefield.

GLOSSARY

boycott–to refuse to buy certain goods

constitution–a country's collection of basic laws

convention–a special meeting

corrupt–likely to use illegal methods to gain power or money

delegate–a person who represents others at a meeting

diplomat–a government official who works with representatives of foreign countries

duty–a tax collected on goods brought into a country from another country

executive branch–the branch of government that carries out laws

grievances–complaints against a person, a group of people, or an organization

judicial branch–the branch of government that makes sure laws are fairly made and carried out

legislative branch–the branch of government that makes laws

merchants–the people who sell goods to the public

militia–a group of citizens who serve as soldiers during an emergency

repeal–to end an existing law

representative–a person chosen to express the views of a large group of people

sedition–words or actions that oppose the government

tyranny–excessive power over people exercised by a ruler or government

writs of assistance–legal documents that allow government officials to search a building

CHRONOLOGY

1735   Born on October 30 in Braintree (later called Quincy), Massachusetts.

1751   Enrolls in Harvard College.

1755   Graduates from Harvard.

1760   Wins his first case as a lawyer.

1763   Publishes his first newspaper article.

1764   Marries Abigail Smith.

1770   Defends British soldiers involved in the Boston Massacre.

1774   Attends First Continental Congress; writes a draft of the Declaration of Rights and Grievances.

1775   Attends Second Continental Congress.

1776   Serves on the committee assigned to write the Declaration of Independence.

1778   Arrives in France to seek aid for America.

1779   Writes a draft of the state constitution for Massachusetts.

1780   Arrives in the Netherlands to seek aid for America.

1783   Signs the Treaty of Paris, which ends the Revolutionary War.

1785   Serves as the first U.S. ambassador to Great Britain.

1786   Publishes first two volumes of *A Defence of the Constitutions of Governments of the United States of America.*

1789   Elected as the first vice president of the United States.

1797   Becomes the second president of the United States.

1798   Signs Alien and Sedition Acts.

1801   Leaves government service and returns to Quincy.

1826   Dies in Quincy on July 4.

REVOLUTIONARY WAR TIME LINE ——

1765 The Stamp Act is passed by the British. Violent protests against it break out in the colonies.

1766 Britain ends the Stamp Act.

1767 Britain passes a law that taxes glass, painter's lead, paper, and tea in the colonies.

1770 Five colonists are killed by British soldiers in the Boston Massacre.

1773 People are angry about the taxes on tea. They throw boxes of tea from ships in Boston Harbor into the water. It ruins the tea. The event is called the Boston Tea Party.

1774 The British pass laws to punish Boston for the Boston Tea Party. They close Boston Harbor. Leaders in the colonies meet to plan a response to these actions.

1775 The Battles of Lexington and Concord begin the American Revolution.

1776 The Declaration of Independence is signed. France and Spain give money to help the Americans fight Britain. Nathan Hale is captured by the British. He is charged with being a spy and is executed.

1777 Leaders choose a flag for America. The American troops win some important battles over the British. General Washington and his troops spend a very cold, hungry winter in Valley Forge.

1778   France sends ships to help the Americans win the war. The British are forced to leave Philadelphia.

1779   French ships head back to France. The French support the Americans in other ways.

1780   Americans discover that Benedict Arnold is a traitor. He escapes to the British. Major battles take place in North and South Carolina.

1781   The British surrender at Yorktown.

1783   A peace treaty is signed in France. British troops leave New York.

1787   The U.S. Constitution is written. Delaware becomes the first state in the Union.

1789   George Washington becomes the first president. John Adams is vice president.

FURTHER READING

Brill, Marlene Targ. *John Adams.* Chicago: Children's Press, 1986.

Egger-Bovet, Howard, and Marlene Smith-Baranzini. *Book of the American Revolution.* Boston: Little, Brown and Company, 1994.

Hakim, Joy. *From Colonies to Country. A History of US,* vol. 3. 2nd rev. ed. New York: Oxford University Press, 1999.

Meeker, Clare Hodgson. *Abigail Adams: Partner in Revolution.* New York: Benchmark Books, 1998.

Meisner, James Jr. *American Revolutionaries and Founders of the Nation.* Berkeley Heights, N.J.: Enslow Publishers, 1999.

Moore, Kay. *If You Lived at the Time of the American Revolution.* New York: Scholastic, 1998.

Smith, Carter, ed. *The Founding Presidents: A Sourcebook on the U.S. Presidency.* Brookfield, Conn.: Millbrook Press, 1995.

INDEX

PICTURE CREDITS

ABOUT THE AUTHOR

As an editor at *Weekly Reader* for six years, **MICHAEL BURGAN** created educational material for an interactive, online service and wrote about current events. Now a freelance author, Michael is a member of the Society of Children's Book Writers and Illustrators and has written more than 30 books for children and young adults. His nonfiction works include a biography of Secretary of State Madeleine Albright; two volumes in the series AMERICAN IMMIGRATION; a book on the history, geography, and culture of Maryland; and shorter books on the Boston Tea Party and the Declaration of Independence. He has a B.A. in history from the University of Connecticut and studied playwriting for one year at Boston's Emerson College.

Senior Consulting Editor **ARTHUR M. SCHLESINGER, JR.** is the leading American historian of our time. He won the Pulitzer Prize for his book *The Age of Jackson* (1945), and again for *A Thousand Days* (1965). This chronicle of the Kennedy Administration also won a National Book Award. He has written many other books, including a multi-volume series, *The Age of Roosevelt.* Professor Schlesinger is the Albert Schweitzer Professor of the Humanities at the City University of New York, and has been involved in several other Chelsea House projects, including the COLONIAL LEADERS series of biographies on the most prominent figures of early American history.